#WERATEDOGS

THE MOST HILARIOUS AND ADORABLE PUPS YOU'VE EVER SEEN

MATT NELSON

Skyhorse Publishing

Skyhorse Publishing books may be purchased in bulk at special discounts for sales promotion, corporate gifts, fund-raising, or educational purposes. Special editions can also be created to specifications. For details, contact the Special Sales Department, Skyhorse Publishing, 307 West 36th Street, 11th Floor, New York, NY 10018 or info@ skyhorsepublishing.com.

Skyhorse® and Skyhorse Publishing® are registered trademarks of Skyhorse Publishing, Inc.®, a Delaware corporation.

Visit our website at www.skyhorsepublishing.com.

10 9 8 7 6 5 4 3

Library of Congress Cataloging-in-Publication Data is available on file.

Cover design by Jenny Zemanek
Cover photographs courtesy of: @Solsjo, @sammmcmanusss, @CayleeErin12, @kerryrite, @jengolbeck, and @jwiley

Print ISBN: 978-1-5107-1714-5
Ebook ISBN: 978-1-5107-1715-2

Printed in China

*Dedicated to good
dogs, far and wide.*

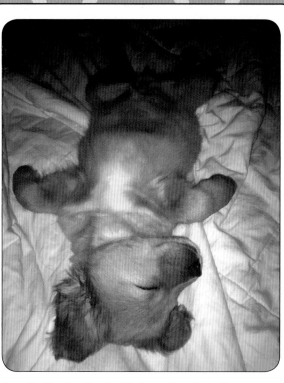

Say hello to Jack. He's quite the sleepy pupper. Thinks he's an airplane. Please make sure your seat backs and tray tables are in their full pupright positions. 12/10 would snug for eternity

Amy Cooper / @alcoopa

This is Holly. She was thoroughly enjoying the flowers until she heard that bees are dying globally at an alarming rate. 11/10 environmentally woke af

Photos courtesy of Courtney Snukis (Holly is currently a service dog in training with Service Dogs by Warren Retrievers)

This is Severus. He's here to fix your Netflix. Looks like he succeeded. Even offered to pupgrade your cable. 13/10 he deserves The Crown

Photos courtesy of Abbie Alcon

Say hello to Lucy. She was just informed that after this walk she can have an ice cube. Lucy has strong feelings towards ice cubes. 12/10

Photo courtesy of Amanda Edwards and Adam Clark

This is Tucker. He kindly requests a hug. 13/10 someone please hug him

Photo courtesy of Caylee Smith

This is Roxy. She paid a photographer to come on a hike with her so she could show her Instagram followers how much she appreciates nature. 11/10 would double tap

Photo courtesy of Lee Pawluk

Meet Louis. He's looking for a h*ck to give. Hasn't found it yet. 13/10

Photo courtesy of Claire Carlson

This is Fezzik. He's a Dark Toned Episcopalian Feta. Fairly common. Avid partaker in late afternoon ball fetching. Would really pupreciate it if you found a way to throw the ball without taking it. 11/10

Photo courtesy of Jocelyn Wicker Draw

This is Meyer. He must hold somebody's hand during all car rides. Also has the most elaborate doggo seatbelt I've ever seen. 12/10 secure af

Photo courtesy of Nina Slaney

This is Penny. She's taking a spontaneous mid-walk snow nap. The best time for a nap, in my opinion. 12/10 would wake when the snow gets too high

Photos courtesy of Mike Evers

This is Baxter. He thrives on casual disinterest. Wears those shades indoors not to prove his undeniable coolness, but to shade his ultimate social uneasiness from an ever-judging world. 12/10

Photo courtesy of Nicole Green and Zach Fuller

This is Scout. He would like a pooch smooch from himself. I'm a strong advocate for loving yourself, but to an extent, Scout. 11/10 h*ckin inappropriate

Photos courtesy of Emma Griffin

This is Champ. He's a self-proclaimed ladies' man secretly in tune with his feelings. Watches "The Bachelorette" to analyze strategy, not for enjoyment. 12/10

Photo courtesy of Patrick Carpenter

This is Gideon. It's his 142nd straight month as best employee. 13/10 well h*ckin deserved

Photos courtesy of @BrewmasterBones

Okay, how did my editor not catch this? We rate dogs, not Yugoslavian Snow Ostriches. Unbelievable. Please be more careful with your submissions next time . . . 11/10 would still pet

Photo submitted by Jayne Soltys, special thanks to Rescue Paws

Say hello to Chompsky. Keychain indicates that his name was chosen independent of these pictures. 13/10 h*ckin intense

Photos courtesy of Jason Wiley

You tried petting the book, didn't you? This is JT (stands for Jesus Twopointoh). He's a Mediterranean Corgicool. 12/10 nice hardwood flooring

Photo courtesy of Nick, Allison, and Jeff Littman of @JTtheCorgi

Like father (doggo), like son (pupper). Both 13/10

Photo courtesy of Jen Golbeck

This is Māui. I've been instructed to tell you that he is, indeed, named after Dwayne Johnson's character in *Moana*. 12/10 would stare into eyes until it's uncomfortable

Photo courtesy of @tannerisntok & @mauiminiaussie

This is Grey. He's the dogtor in charge of your checkpup today. 12/10 would never miss an appointment

Photos courtesy of Kelsey Davis

This is Bella. She's looking for love. Been at it for a while. I asked her if she considered lowering her standards. She said not a chance in h*ck. 13/10

Photo courtesy of Bella's BFF Jilly

This is Dave. He's in a predicament. Doesn't seem to mind though. Just hanging out. 12/10 someone please assist Dave

Photo courtesy of Kendall A. Freeman

Meet Otto. He's a Cumulostratus Floofus. Certifiably fluffy af. Randomly bursts into song. 12/10 would harmonize

SIDE NOTE: Floofuses are usually born with a turtleneck sweater already on

Instagram @OttoVonEskie

Meet Django. He accidentally opened the front-facing camera. Seems to have done him quite the frighten. 12/10 Background dog receives an 11/10 for her honorable obliviousness

Photo courtesy of The Traskos Family

This is Blaire. These are her senior pics. Everybody knows candid is cooler. Struggled to go five seconds without trying to eat her backdrop. Still, 12/10 would leave an Insta comment

Photos courtesy of Lydia Bruns and Family

This is Corona. She discovered the only way makeup should be tested on animals. Groundbreaking as h*ck. 11/10 would continue testing

Photo courtesy of Carley Frier

27

Say hello to Klein. He looks like a DreamWorks character. These pictures were taken one month apart. He knows he's a stud now. 13/10 would let him break my heart

Photos courtesy of Luana Soare

I'm not sure how this keeps happening. We only rate dogs. Please don't send non-canines like this Bangladeshi Couch Chipmunk. Thank you . . . 12/10

Photo courtesy of Kristen and Mike Santee

29

This is Buddy. He's a Sicilian Gouda. Exotic as h*ck. 12/10 unbelievably huggable

Photo courtesy of @superlau77

This is Mister. He's an incredible father. Always takes time out of his day to play with his sons. 13/10 heartwarming af

Photos courtesy of Nick Ray (IG: @Nick_Ray Twitter: @Nick_ray97)

This caption is completely irrelevant. Just look at how h*ckin adorable this pupper is. The name is Layla. 13/10

Photos courtesy of Bailey Eslick, Phoenix AZ

This is Toby. He just got to the climax of his scary story. One can assume all listeners are frightened af. 12/10 tone it down a notch, Toby

Photo courtesy of Casey and Sarah M

Meet Larry. He has no self-control. Nifty tongue slip though. 12/10

Photos courtesy of Hanna Hall

This is Ellie. She's studying to be the best doggo she can be. 13/10 future valedogtorian

Photos courtesy of Brittany Booth

This is Charlie. He embraces winter. Extra treats for whoever can find the snowflake heart. 11/10 would hug for warmth

Photos courtesy of Abbigail Nelson

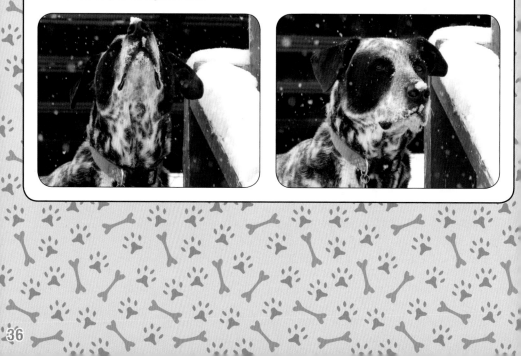

Say hello to Rocky. He got triple-doggo-dared. Bamboozled, if you will. Now he's properly stuck af. 11/10 someone help him

Photo courtesy of Dan Morrow

Say hello to Romeo. He was just told it's too cold for the pool. H*ckin nonsense. 11/10 would help fill pup

Photos courtesy of Emanuelle DaSilva (Instagram: whoanelly)

This is Maverick. He's checking for monsters under your bed. Just wants you to feel safe. 13/10 super good boy

Photo courtesy of Morgan P. Tanner

Say hello to Tove. She's a Luxembourgian Hazelnut Flop. Ferocious breed. Can be extremely lethal. Puppears to be wearing socks. Perhaps for extra traction when she pounces. 12/10 would pet with extreme caution

Photo courtesy of Benjamin Mooney

Meet Cooper. He just got out of the pupper hospital. Beat the h*ck out of Parvo. It didn't stand a chance against him. 13/10 fearless af

Photos courtesy of Amanda Collins & Sweet Family

This is Moose. In the first picture, he's making sure his owner doesn't leave for college without him. In the second, he's making sure you know how h*ckin ridiculous his ears are. I bet he trips over them sometimes. 12/10 would flap ears to give the illusion of flight

Photos courtesy of John A. Gardner

Meet Lincoln. His eyes are magic and his nose looks like the night sky. 12/10 would hug softly

Photos courtesy of Nina Velichka

Say hello to Butter. She can have whatever she wants forever. 12/10 would snug so well

Photo courtesy of Eric Blake

This is Hefner. He's fancy af. Eats more carrots than other dogs. Hops at random. Very mediocre at fetch. Still fun to hug. 11/10 would take home to Mom

Photo courtesy of Mari Nelson Photography

Say hello to Finley. She's a Beneboop
Cumbersplash. The curliest of Beneboops.
12/10 would commit atrocities for

Photo courtesy of Ty and Sarah Eblen

Meet Gus. I'm told he's a six-time world champion cuddler. No need to fact check that. 11/10 would share chair with

Photo courtesy of Catherine Warrick

This is Blue. Someone just told him that cats are better than dogs. H*ckin hilarious. 12/10

Photos courtesy of JD Kinniburgh

Meet Coco. She's listening for the mailman. Can usually hear him put on his shoes in the morning. 12/10 dedicated af

Photo courtesy of Kate Linn

This is Zeke. It's his first snow. He's never experienced anything like it. Pupset because he thinks it's just his dandRUFF shampoo not working. 12/10 it's fine Zeke, everything's fine

Photos courtesy of Trinity Parker

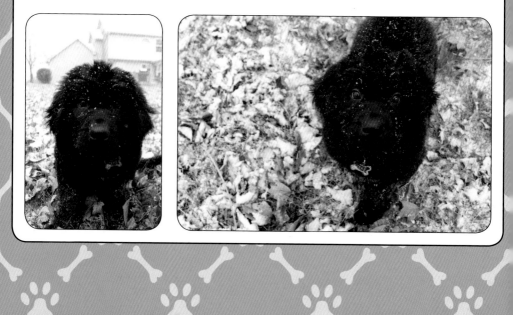

This is Leo. A caterpillar just crawled in his ear. Deep breaths Leo. It's going to be okay. 12/10 would comfort

Photo courtesy of Laura Drayton

Meet Chevy. He had a late breakfast and now must choose between a late lunch and an early dinner. 11/10 understandably pupset

Photo courtesy of Ashley Brown

This is Jess. She's quite feisty. Ready to box. About to hit you with a powerful puppercut to the chin. Pound for hound best boxer in the region. 13/10 would ask before petting

Photo courtesy of Jordan Thornquest

Say hello to Milo. I would do terrible, terrible things for Milo. 13/10

Photo courtesy of Kara Giles

This is Beau. He loves carrots and now he knows that the carrots love him too. 12/10

Photos courtesy of Savanna Argenti (@savi_js)

Say hello to Bazil Goldberg. Her head is fantastically dispupportionate. Must be super h*ckin rare. Seems to be fully aware of how perfect she is. 13/10 would be an honor to pet

Photo courtesy of @baziltheblueheelercorgi

This is Apollo. He would like you to accept this rose. We should introduce him to Bella from earlier. Matchmaker af. 13/10 someone please accept Apollo's rose

Photo courtesy of Chelsea Linaweaver

Meet Cooper. He likes to stick his tongue out at you and then laugh about it. 12/10 quite the jokester

Photos courtesy of Hannah and Lucy Williams

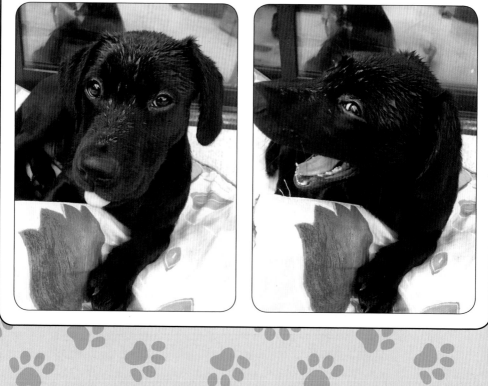

This is Sunshine. She likes to get pup close and personal. Sneaky tongue slip, though. Eyes far apart for a dog. Forehead is basically a weapon. Would still boop. 11/10 would pet with wonder

Photo courtesy of Whitney Smith

This is Wallace. You said you brushed your teeth but he checked your toothbrush and it was bone-dry. 11/10 not pupset, just disappointed

Photo courtesy of Elizabeth McNair

Say hello to Gabe and Ava. They are the best of friends. Gabe can't talk yet, but neither can Ava, so it's okay. 11/10 for Ava and an honorary 11/10 for tiny human pupper Gabe

Photos courtesy of Sarah and Brett Armstrong

This is Daisy. She's simply here to make you smile. If you're having a bad day, it is now less bad. 12/10 mission h*ckin successful

Photo courtesy of Mallory Hladik

This is getting ridiculous. We only rate dogs. Please don't send in any more Wild Albanian Street Moose. Thank you . . . 11/10

Photo courtesy of Susanne Sjöstedt

Meet Pancake. She winks better than you do. Also has a snazzy Batman bandana. 13/10 she's the pupper we need, but not the pupper we deserve

Photo courtesy of Samantha McManus (@sammcmanusss)

This is Tyrone. He's a leaf wizard. Not even he knows the full extent of his power. He has no eyes though. Every hero has a weakness, I guess. Inspirational af. 13/10 enthusiasm is tangible

Photos courtesy of Victoria Riggins

This is Nora. You said she couldn't touch her toes. She maintained eye contact while she proved you wrong. Pupset you would ever doubt her. 12/10 would pat head approvingly

Photo courtesy of Christina Dowling

Really? Again? We only rate dogs. This . . . is a Taiwanese Guide Walrus. Please only send dogs. Thank you. 11/10

Photo courtesy of Serena Monteiro

This is Minnie. She's an exceptionally fluffy pup. Had a little Valentine's photo shoot this year. The shade's bring the whole outfit together. 12/10 would hug for a while

Photos courtesy of Kaitlin Gold

This is Davey. He'll have your daughter home by eight. A real stand up pup. 11/10 would introduce to Mom

Photo courtesy of Amy Mackey

This is Moreton. He's the Good Boy Who Lived. Solemnly swears he's up to lots of good. 9¾/10 magical as h*ck

Photos courtesy of Krista Thomas

This is Luna. Her eyes are prepped to get lost in. She's also very powerful. Carries that moose around all day. He's got a bum leg and can't get around well. That's where Luna steps in. Heroic af. 13/10 would pet well

Photo courtesy of @MHolcomb14

This is Bailey. She loves going down slides but her technique could use some work. Background doggo seems to be a coach of sorts. Maybe just present for moral support. 11/10 for both

Photos courtesy of Savannah Carpenter

Meet Sedona. This picture was taken from the feed of a skier's GoPro as she saved him from an avalanche. True story. Probably. 13/10 pupple heart worthy

Photo courtesy of Danielle Priebe (Instagram: @sedona_thegoldenpup)

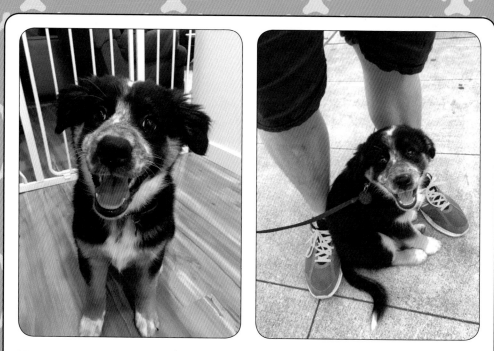

This is Rizzy. She's a Triscuitarian Cheddar. Known for their contagious smiles. 12/10 would smile back

Photos courtesy of Sally Taylor, St. Clair

This is Lennon. He's a Boopershnoop Pupperdoop. Quite rare. Exceptionally pettable. 12/10 would definitely boop that shnoop

Photo courtesy of Larisa and John Richards

This is Ollie Vue. He was a three-legged pupper on a mission to overcome everything. He touched the heart of everyone who heard his story. 14/10 we will miss you Ollie

Photo courtesy of @ollievuesomuch

This is Eevie. Her tongue slippage does not rest, even when she does. 12/10 would attempt to boop without waking

Photos courtesy of The Kilpatricks

This is Milo. You just woke him. His wake pup routine consists of an impeccable stretch/yawn combination. Downright h*ckin puptastic. 13/10 would snug well

Photo courtesy of Kelly Gale

Say hello to Ellie. Try not to do her a frighten, though. She's becoming one with the wilderness . . . or she's stuck. 12/10 would support her either way

Photos courtesy of @gather

This is Oshie. He's ready to party. Nobody knows how he scored the case. Must have a fake. Was seen later that night trying to shotgun a can of Spaghettios. 12/10 sign me pup to party with Oshie

Photo courtesy of @oshiegoldenbear

Meet Walter. He's actually two dogs fused together. 13/10 innovative as h*ck

Photo courtesy of Vincent Iadevaia

This is Neiko. He was brutally ambushed by leaves. Fortunately, he caught one for further questioning. Has never encountered such a spook. Doesn't want it happening again. 13/10

Photos courtesy of Shelby Kleiman and Bailey Dalton

Say hello to Audi. She is an elder doggo. Exudes wisdom. Hairy feet are simply immaculate. Bone themed leash is very fitting for a dog. 12/10 would give infinite pats

Photo courtesy of Audi's mom, Rita Slawinski

Here lies Chelsea. I see three pawsible explanations for her current fluid-like state. She wasn't properly assembled, she's consciously trying to conserve space for the convenience of those around her, or she forgot how to dog. 11/10 we may never know

Photo courtesy of Audrey H. Dittman

This is Ysera. According to her owner, she is a doofus who likes to eat rocks, but I see more. I see a doggo with dreams yet to be discovered. Endless pawsibilities in every direction. 13/10 never give pup

Photo courtesy of Ysera Siegman

Meet Bandit. He was having the grandest of times adventuring until a leaf landed on his noggin. Has no clue what to do next. Wait it out, I guess. 11/10 would comfort throughout this inpupportune time

Photos courtesy of Samantha Houde

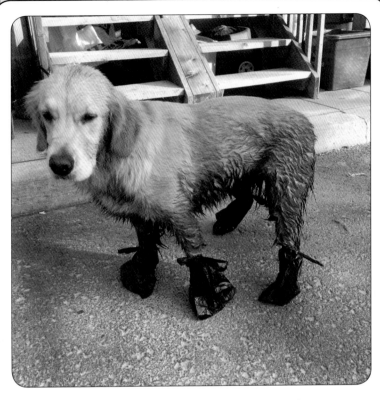

This is Hattie. She had an amazing time in the mud, but was swiftly denied the satisfaction of destroying the house with it. Certifiably pupset. 12/10 would console with pets

Photo courtesy of Jamine Ackert (@capitalyoga)

This is Tobillo. She's properly fetching her shot and simultaneously outshining the morning sun. 13/10 would send a fully armed battalion to remind her of my love

Photo courtesy of Lin-Manuel Miranda

Say hello to Poco. He's a pretty pointy pupper. Perfectly portable. Seems kind of evil. Not entirely convinced Poco isn't plotting some sort of world domination. Still, 10/10 would keep in frocket

Photos courtesy of Maura Hennelly

Meet Larry. I think it's safe to say he's found his stick. H*ckin pleased with it. 13/10 euphoric af

Photos courtesy of Brian Weber

Meet Finnegan. He doesn't know why you are on one side of the barrier and he is on the other, but he would like these circumstances to change. Requests a switch pup. 12/10

Photo courtesy of @catrhoda

This is Ace. He's being raised pup Simba style to indicate his importance. Floof level off the charts. 12/10 would worship

Photo courtesy of @the.patriots.pups on Instagram

This is Odie. He's big. 13/10 would attempt to ride. Background doggo incredibly shook.

Photos courtesy of Michelle Brooke

This is Snicku. He's having trouble reading because he's a dog. Glasses only helped a little. Also, that's a dictionary. Nap preferred. 12/10 sleep tight puppo

Photos courtesy of Mansi Goyal

Meet Oscar. It's his birthday. He doesn't know that though. He just knows that once in a while he gets a bunch of extra pets, an extra walk, and a pointlessly aesthetically pleasing treat conglomerate. 11/10 happy birthday Oscar

Photo courtesy of Julia Fox

Say hello to Atlas. He's a legend, to put it lightly. Here he is showcasing his floof and revolutionizing tongue slip. 13/10 would be an honor to pet

Photos courtesy of @everythingatlas on Instagram

Say hello to Doug. He's a Brazilian Corgiclap. Proud of his heritage. Obsessed with soccer. Pupseveres even with the whole tiny leg thing. 12/10 admirable af

Photo courtesy of Meredith Melton

Are you h*ckin kidding me? Another one? Please stop sending in non-canines like this Mongolian grass snake. We only rate dogs. This is very frustrating . . . 11/10

Photo courtesy of Jamie Crowley

Say hello to Blue. She's just gorgeous and so is this picture and I wanted you all to see it. 13/10 dazzling af

Photo courtesy of Chandler Benthal/submission courtesy of Natalia Benthal

This is Chester. He demands to play Patty Cake. No petting until it has been completed. 11/10 inspiring paw-eye coordination

Photo courtesy of Eve Moore

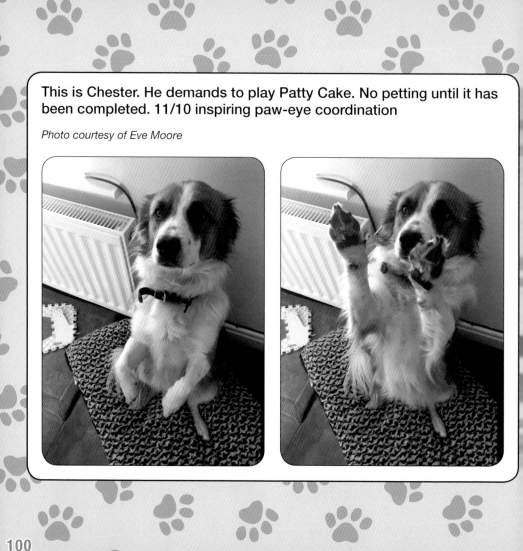

Meet Fitz. He can't believe his own tongue. Wondering if such a tongue is standard for a puppo of his kind. It's a rather insane oral puppendage, Fitz, but I think you'll be okay. 12/10

Photo courtesy of Kristin Craw (@KristinCraw)

This is Tucker.
His ball seems to
think he's naughty,
but Tucker knows
better than that.
Verified good boy.
11/10 would boop
then pet

*Photo courtesy of Jake
Osborne (@JakeOs1234)*

Meet Fizz. She believes love is a social construct consisting solely of ideals perpetuated by mass media. 11/10 woke af

Photos courtesy of Esther Jordinson

This is Derek. He puppears to be extraordinarily huggable. Just had a blue pupsicle as well. 12/10 would snug intensely

Photo courtesy of Lisa Balla

Meet Akumi. He was left outside for 30 minutes. Seems to have found a friend. Already named it Steve. 13/10 for both Akumi and Steve

Photo courtesy of Candyce Wu

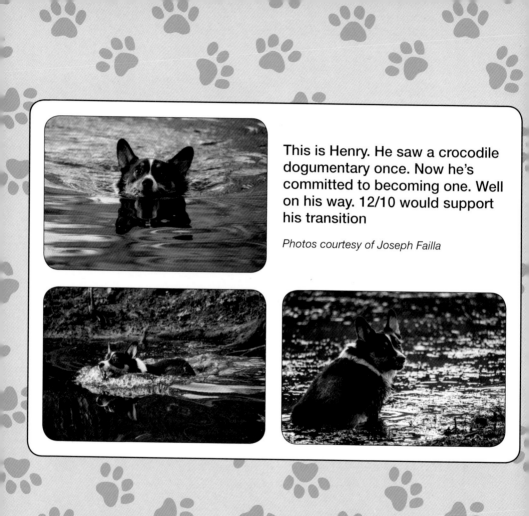

This is Henry. He saw a crocodile dogumentary once. Now he's committed to becoming one. Well on his way. 12/10 would support his transition

Photos courtesy of Joseph Failla

This is Moose. It looks like he just asked you to do something daring with him and is trying to convince you that there's no way it's illegal. 12/10 would probably succumb to the pup peer pressure

Photo courtesy of Joe Naughton

This is Tyr. He is pupturbed by the current state of traffic. He has a Christmas brunch to get to. How else will people see his h*ckin adorable sweater. 12/10 one could say he's a top-Tyr pupper

Photo courtesy of Sarah and Josh Brewer

Say hello to Juneau. Her ears puppear to be exceptional and we're here to recognize them. 12/10 would rub against my face

Photo courtesy of Jason Bode

This is Anakin. He strives to reach his full doggo potential. Tragically, he was born with a blurry tail. Despite this inherent disadvantage, he persists. 13/10 role model af

Doggo courtesy of Lucy James, Scott Preedy, and Sam Preedy/Photo courtesy of Niall Van Santen

Meet Esko. He has a secret Winnie-the-Pooh addiction. Addicted to the profound wisdom and timeless quotes that left a multigenerational mark on humanity, that is. Nothing to be ashamed of, Esko. 11/10 would definitely pet

Photo courtesy of Jillian and Richard

This is Zelda. She's a model for Dogue. Doin a brief tongue slip on the bridge. H*ckin photogenic. 11/10

Photos courtesy of Sam Himburg

Say hello to Olly. He's an intellectual. Whatever you're saying clearly doesn't interest him. Itching to get back to calculating how many treats could stick to the outside of a tennis ball if it were covered in peanut butter. 13/10

Photo courtesy of Sam Sheldon

This is Silver. It's time for her first walk ever and she just saw how much h*ckin snow there was. Not impressed. 12/10 would puppreciate some warmth in the paw area

Photos courtesy of @syddanngiess

Meet Nala. Today, she preferred the pantry to a walk, and that's okay. Puppos may choose their own adventure. 12/10 would still snug

Photo courtesy of Marshall Denny

Meet Sunny. He can take down a polar bear in one fell swoop. Fr*cken deadly af. More of a threat than climate change. 13/10 would pet with the pupmost respect

Photos courtesy of the Whitley Family

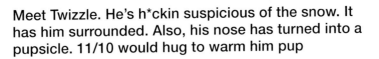

Meet Twizzle. He's h*ckin suspicious of the snow. It has him surrounded. Also, his nose has turned into a pupsicle. 11/10 would hug to warm him pup

Photo courtesy of Jeanne Poull

Say hello to Ollie. As soon as your eyes adjust to him and his snazzy tie, he switches it pup. Boom, new basket, new tie. Always puppared. Nothing comes between Ollie and looking dapper af. 13/10

Photos courtesy of Sarah and Amy Goodman

This is Lancelot. He's doing what's known in the industry as a powdery tongue hang. Trying to collect those good flakes. Also has some majestic eyes. 11/10 would pet firmly

Photos courtesy of Monica Enriquez

Meet Karsten. This is her first time skiing. Don't worry doggo, we'll get you some doggles to go with that festive af bandana. 11/10 would pet all over the slopes

Photo courtesy of Madison Cox and @ Karsten_the_Bernese

This is Maple. She knows not to stare at certain soapy floating orbs directly after the whole Kenneth situation. May he one day be free. Maple will let the bubble hover past her in solidarity. 11/10 be strong, Maple, be strong for Kenneth

Photo courtesy of Megan DeRocher

This is Leo. It's his birthday. Probably not while you're reading this, but when the picture was taken. His bow tie is unbelievably nifty. Only partially disrupted by constant tongue slippage. 13/10 would pay to pet

Photo courtesy of Matthew Teal

Meet Mak. These pictures were taken a year apart. He may get bigger, but his respect for personal space remains the same. 12/10 would boop in both instances

Photos courtesy of Danielle Keysor

This was Lilo. She was a firm believer in blind fishing. Thought catching the fish was too easy if you were looking, so she did it with her eyes closed. Tongue out is a sign of focus. 13/10 RIP Lilo

Photos courtesy of Friends of Lilo: Iiris, Heli, Maija, Venla, and Maukka

This is Sam.
You can tell he
has big dreams.
And that he will
follow them.
12/10 change
the h*ckin
world, pupper

*Photo courtesy of
Mark Stanton*

This is Lennon. He's just h*ckin gorgeous. Almost intimidatingly so. 13/10 would pet in amazement

Photo courtesy of @lennon_official/@ideaform

This is Theodore. It looks like he's done something naughty and is now locked pup. Seems to feel bad about it though. 11/10 would puppeal court decision

Photo courtesy of @theodore_retriever

This is Liberty. I was told she loves America and barking at birds. She also puppears to be an expert selfie-taker. 11/10 would snap back

Photos courtesy of @amandaneibauer

This is Kira. She's pretty pupset with you. Would like to be removed from this soapy, wet h*ck. Her left ear gives off a friendly vibe, but her right ear means business. 12/10 would dry off then pet

Photo courtesy of Erin M.

Meet Ochre. She destroyed her friend. She isn't sure why she did it. It felt good at the time. 11/10 would buy Ochre a new toy to cheer her pup

Photo courtesy of Cassandra Trissler

This is Mulligan. His hobbies include swinging and being adorable while swinging. Kindly requests a push. 12/10 would happily oblige

Photo courtesy of Lauren Deppe and Sarah Asseng

This is Matt. He has constructed a machine that clones a slightly smaller version of himself. Innovative as h*ck. 13/10 please use the machine on the smaller version to make an even smaller version

Photos courtesy of Fernanda Bertasso

Say hello to Scout. He's a firm believer in the beach. Thinks the water is the biggest puddle ever and the beach is just a squishy yard. 11/10 would perform a sandy boop

Photo courtesy of Sarah-Anne Winchester/taken by Rebecca-Joy Winchester

Meet Bradley. He did a splish and splash. Like an honest Ryan Lochte. Only got in to make sure you were safe. 13/10 super good boy

Photos courtesy of @nickwolfson

This is Harlso. He made breakfast for you. Didn't know what to do with the egg though. Couldn't crack it without thumbs. Valiant effort still. 13/10 would attempt to eat without disrupting balance

Instagram @harlso_the_balancing_hound

This is Schmidt. He's doing a standard swift mlem. Got it in right before the important pic. Scarf is officially nifty as h*ck. 12/10 seasonally puppropriate af

Photos courtesy of Alyssa Al-Chokhachi

This is Archie. He's an incredibly rare Rainbow-Cheeked Doggo. One of seven in existence. 13/10 would pet cheek first

Photo courtesy of Victoria (@YouMeAtHalf5)

This is Sampson. He just graduated. Puppared to be a doggo now. Time for the real world. 12/10 have fun with taxes

Photos courtesy of Mary DeSimone

Say hello to Beau and Wilbur. Wilbur has stolen Beau's bed. He now has so much room for activities. His smugness is reaching never-before-seen levels. Beau is, needless to say, pupset with these new developments. 12/10 for both

Photo courtesy of Heidi Anderson

This is Tucker. He spends his days bustin h*ckin ghosts. Currently making sure you're not a ghost. Dedicated af. 13/10 I feel safe in Tucker's presence

Photo courtesy of Josh Manning

Say hello to Finn. He's doing a head-on tongue slip. Not so sneaky. Seems to be requesting reassurance that he's a good boy. 12/10 can confirm good boy status

Photo courtesy of Mattie Boyett (Finn's Momma)

This is Axxel and Dexter. They found the one big rock among the colorful little rocks. Decided it was a superb settling location and set pup camp. Both 12/10 would pet simultaneously

Photos courtesy of Jennifer Burke

This is Bernie. He's a Croatian Pewterschmidt. One of the sturdier breeds. I seem to not be able to stop looking at his feet. 12/10 would hug softly

Photo courtesy of Jennifer Pryor

This is Jimison. He's on the larger side when it comes to puppers. Still sporting one h*ck of a tounge slip. Fairly long face. Needs a haircut for sure. Still, 11/10 would pet cautiously

Photo courtesy of Sara Moore

This is Niko. He kindly requested a boop, and he got one. H*ckin satisfied. 13/10 same time tomorrow

Photos courtesy of Jordan Walts

Say hello to Winnie. She accidentally opened the front-facing camera, but then realized she's flawless and proceeded to take more pictures. 13/10 confident af

Photos courtesy of Erin Calder/Winnie is a guide doggo in training with @ GuideDogs

Meet BeBe. She rocks the messy bun of your dreams. H*ckin flawless. 12/10 would watch her tutorial

Photo courtesy of Nick Gaudio & Verity Bell (Instagram: @bebethespaniel)

Meet Harley. He's quite the cheeky puppo. Manages to expose his tongue in all four photos. That's unheard of in this industry. 13/10 h*ckin remarkable

Photos courtesy of Ben Dalrymple

This is Remi. He has waited all afternoon for a pupportunity to lick the snow without any witnesses. Mission successful. 12/10

Photo courtesy of Codi Foster

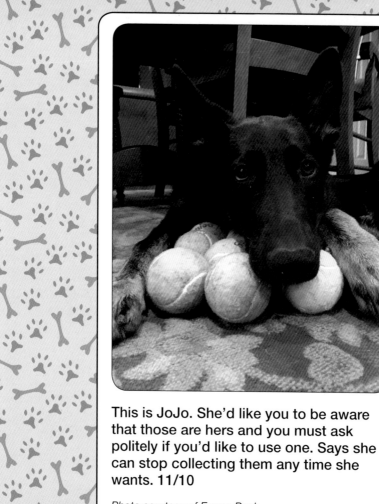

This is JoJo. She'd like you to be aware that those are hers and you must ask politely if you'd like to use one. Says she can stop collecting them any time she wants. 11/10

Photo courtesy of Emma Peck

This is Chief. He put the bow on himself as a symbol. Wants everyone to know that he is a gift to this household and to start treating him with some respect. 12/10 take a breather, Chief, we all love you

Photos courtesy of Taylor Rolfe and Levi Fortner

This is Maycee. She was thoroughly enjoying the snow until her ear got turned inside out. Doesn't know how to fix it. 12/10 someone help her

Photos courtesy of Lauren Murphy

Say hello to Bailey. She matches the leaves around her. Aesthetic as h*ck. 11/10

Photos courtesy of Anna Richardson

Meet Penny. She fought a bee and lost. 11/10 it's fine Penny, everything's fine

Photo courtesy of Carrie Rosol

This is Nollie. She found out today that she adores the beach. Also, portable as h*ck. If you don't wave back to her you're a monster. 13/10

Photos courtesy of BJ Holt (@breightysucks)

This is Harper. She scraped her elbow attempting a backflip off a tree. Pointing to where it hurts. Valiant effort though. 12/10 would kiss it until it's better

Photo courtesy of Brittany Hendrix

This is Jim. He's very nervous. Not sure if you're going to be gone five minutes or forever. He knows better than to worry about these things, but he can't help it. 11/10 I'll always come back for you, Jim

Photos courtesy of Jim's best friend

Meet Finn. He's doing one h*ck of a snooze. I wonder what he's dreaming about. Probably pupper things. 12/10 would attempt to boop without waking

Photos courtesy of Erica and Shelby Rogers

Say hello to Stubert. He just arrived.
Batteries not included. 11/10 has that new
doggo smell

Photo courtesy of Parul Kapoor

This is Vela. She doesn't give a h*ck about the law. Could care less about your precious stipupupations. Churlish, but in an admirable way. 12/10 free-willed af

Photo courtesy of Eva Snyder

This is Genevieve. She just got her ears crimped. Trying to be one of the more stylish puppers around. 12/10 would snug passionately

Photo courtesy of Michael and Sandy Wise

Say hello to Scout. He's fixated on a cloud that looks like a mailman. Completely understandable. 12/10 would follow him anywhere

Instagram @vikingpupscout

This is Charlie. He pouts until he gets to go on the swing. It works flawlessly and always will. 12/10 adorably manipulative af

Photos courtesy of Tre Puccinelli

This is Kirby. He's being sassy as h*ck. Knows you only pretended to throw that ball last time. Wants you to promise you're not going to do that again. 12/10 no more bamboozling

Photo courtesy of Amanda Linzalone and Olivia Roberds

Meet Tiggy. He's playing hide-and-seek. It's his turn to seek. Not the best counter, but that's okay. 12/10 definitely peeking

Photo courtesy of Alan Atkinson

Have you collected yourself? Okay. This is Dublin. He's underinflated and it makes him look a thousand years old. 13/10 would snug so well

Photo courtesy of Bailey Wright

This is Ryder. He doesn't actually know how to surf. Uses the board to pick pup babes in the ocean. Almost too easy. 13/10 surfs pup

Photo courtesy of @alyssaweymann

This is Logan. The photographer was being paid to take pictures of that couple in the background, but then Logan happened. Couldn't resist. 12/10 I think these turned out great

Photos courtesy of Chelsea Saxman

This is Atticus. He'd like you to wake pup now. You have a lot on your schedule today including hopefully several walks followed by intimate belly rubs. 12/10

Photo courtesy of Antonio Javiniar (@atticusky)

This is Kono. She swears she took off a few pounds.
Scale must be messed pup. 12/10 new collar must
weigh more

Photo courtesy of Hannah Venus

This is Lilly. She just parallel barked. Kindly requests a reward now. Don't forget to buckle pup. 13/10 would pet so well

Photo courtesy of Alexandra Herndon

This is Max. He's actually hovering over the snow. Doesn't touch the ground once. 11/10 magical af

Photos courtesy of Morgan Marostega Photography

Meet Rossi. He's addicted to smelling flowers. It's tearing his family apart. Won't even admit he has a problem. Still, 11/10 would help him help himself

Photos courtesy of Brooke LeVan

Say hello to Sundance. He thoroughly enjoys pizza. Won't put it down for anything. 13/10 frighteningly relatable

Photo courtesy of Sweet Sundance

This is Kade. He put his hood pup so you know he means business. Puppared to battle. Unfortunately for Kade, both him and his friend are too adorable to take seriously. 12/10 would battle some other time

Photos courtesy of Michaela Vanderhaeghan

Meet Cooper. Someone just told him that Snape kills Dumbledore. C'mon Cooper. It's not a spoiler if it's been eight years. 12/10 would console

Photos courtesy of Jordan Thomas and @coop__the__golden

Unbelievable . . . We. Only. Rate. Dogs. Not unevenly toasted marshmallows. Please only submit dogs. Again, cannot believe my editor didn't catch it. 13/10 would still pet

Photo courtesy of Rachel Borowski/taken by Ray Borowski

This is Roscoe. He's so aware of how photogenic he is that he tries to mess pup photos. Throws in a cheeky yawn or an uneasy smile to give the impression of imperfection. 11/10 you're not fooling anyone Roscoe

Photos courtesy of Maddy Vue

This is Buddy. Car rides excite him because he knows an adventure is about to happen. Don't forget to buckle pup. 12/10 would've been 13, but I can't encourage unsafe puppo habits

Photo courtesy of Ric Wallis

This is Daphne. Every day she puts on that costume and watches the same wild chickens visit her yard, desperately hoping to be accepted. She just wants some friends. 13/10 maybe one day, Daphne

Photo courtesy of E. Wang and C. Fleitas

This is Dexter. He's doing his trademarked pupside down smile. Thinks regular smiles are boring. 12/10 good boy status achieved

Photo courtesy of Brianna Dillon

Say hello to Madeline. She's got some of the greatest flip-pup sunglasses in existence. Convenience and aesthetic have never been combined in a more aggressively average way. 11/10

Photo courtesy of Laura Abigail

This is Bruno. The longer you look at him, the more you see past his majestic exterior and into the soul of a troubled doggo. One that is seeking a puppose outside of just being a "good boy." He wants to be . . . the best boy. 13/10

Photo courtesy of Jeremiah Krueger

This is Ophie. She couldn't help herself. The low-hanging stick with the pretty colors was too tempting for her to ignore. 11/10 completely understandable

Photos courtesy of Kelsi Brinkmeyer

This is Donut. She's a sled doggo. Decided it was much more fun to be pulled rather than do the pulling. Wondering why she didn't figure this out a while ago. 12/10

Photo courtesy of Chrissie Bodznick

This is Terry. He doesn't mean to bother you. Was just wondering if you have any snacks. It's okay if you don't, he figured he'd ask anyway. 11/10 h*ckin polite doggo

Photo courtesy of Ellie Doyen (@El_0h_Ellie)

This is Zeke. His main passion is leaves. World-class when it comes to eating them. 12/10 precious as h*ck

Instagram: @zeke_likes_leaves

Say hello to Toby. He's a Hungarian Speckle-Eared Rutabaga. Quite rare. One magical eye. Clearly had braces at one point. Wore retainer religiously. 12/10 handsome af

Photo courtesy of Javier A.

This is Gump. That's his chair. He labeled it so everyone's aware. Wouldn't want any mix-pups. 12/10 pupperly attributed af

Photo courtesy of Calista Porter

Meet Ralph, like Dexter, he prefers the pupside down smile. He likes the feeling of gravity on his tongue. Incredibly susceptible to belly rubs. 11/10 would rub belly

Photo courtesy of Kaitlyn Gill

This is my dog. Her name is Zoey. She knows I've been rating other dogs. She's not happy. 13/10 no bias at all

Photo courtesy of the DogFather

THE DOGTIONARY

dog•go
/'dôgō/
noun

1. A big pupper, usually older. This label does not stop a doggo from behaving like a pupper.
2. A pupper that appears to have its life in order. Probably understands taxes and whatnot.

"That's a really good doggo."
"I give my doggo a firm pat every night before bed."

pup•per
/'pəpər/
noun

1. A small doggo, usually younger. Can be equally, if not more mature than some doggos.
2. A doggo that is inexperienced, unfamiliar, or in any way unprepared for the responsibilities associated with being a doggo.

"H*ck, that's one pettable pupper."
"How many puppers could I fit on my body at once, if I were lying down?"

pup•po
/ˈpəpō/
noun

1. A transitional phase between pupper and doggo. Easily understood as the dog equivalent of a teenager.
2. A dog with a mixed bag of both pupper and doggo tendencies.

"My puppo is still learning what it takes to be a trustworthy doggo."
"I would hug that puppo so passionately."

blep
/ˈblep/
verb

1. An extremely subtle act that occurs without the knowledge of the one who slips. The act includes one's tongue protruding ever so slightly from the mouth, usually just noticeable enough that it attracts the attention it deserves. Can last between three seconds and four days.

"My doggo did a h*ck of a blep the other day."
"Get a load of this blep I captured."

mlem
/mˈlem/
verb

1. An act of extending and retracting one's tongue in a casual manner, perhaps to acquire a substance around the mouth or even on the tongue itself. Not to be confused with a blep, a mlem is more dynamic and can occur multiple times over the standard duration of a blep.

"Mlem, mlem, mlem."
"To obtain the peanut butter on his snoot, my dog did several mlems in a row."

boop
/boop/
verb
1. To lightly, but enthusiastically touch with forefinger, usually on the nose.
2. An act of intimacy that can be rejected or accepted by the individual being booped.

"I've never seen a snoot I wouldn't boop."
"I wasn't interested in whether the owner liked me or not, but the dog accepted my boop, so all was well."

snoot
/snoot/
noun

1. The nose of a dog. Usually found in places the dog may not fit. The location of the snoot may hint at where the dog's interest lies.

"That is a beautiful snoot."
"I've been trying to boop my neighbor's dog's snoot for six years."

floof
/floof, floof/
noun

1. Any dog really. However, this label is commonly given to dogs with seemingly excess fur. Comical amounts of fur on a dog will certainly earn the dog this generic name.
2. Dog fur. The term holds true whether the fur is still on the dog, or if it has been shed off.

"Check out that majestic floof!"
"The floof on my dog has gotten out of control but I don't see anybody complaining any time soon."

h*ck
/hek/
exclamation

1. A non-aggressive placeholder for more vulgar exclamations. Used frequently because dogs evoke so much emotion from humans every time they do literally anything.

"I love dogs with every h*ckin fiber of my being."
"H*ck!"

bam•boo•zle
/bam'boozəl/
verb

1. The act of confusing a dog, whether intentional or not. It does not take much, but can be done strategically. Recovery time for the dog can vary, but you're usually looking at at least fifteen seconds of preoccupation. Things dogs are commonly bamboozled by include: glass, fake ball throwing, changes of surface, any noise ever, trigonometry, etc.

"My dog was thoroughly bamboozled when I switched his food and water bowls."

"Bamboozle your dog by getting a slightly smaller version of him and then giving the small one more attention."

zoom

/zoom/

noun

1. A very speedy move done by a dog. Incredibly hard to document, but
   universally recognized as a thing that happens. Appears to break laws
   of physics, but only because when your dog does something average,
   you think it is the greatest thing ever.

"That was a h*ck of a zoom!"

"My dog does a zoom whenever the doorbell rings."